HEARTS AMOK: A MEMOIR IN VERSE

HEARTS AMOK:

A MEMOIR IN VERSE

KEVIN SPENST

ANVIL PRESS / VANCOUVER

Anvil Press Publishers Inc.
P.O. Box 3008, Main Post Office
Vancouver, B.C. V6B 3X5 CANADA
www.anvilpress.com

Library and Archives Canada Cataloguing in Publication

Title: Hearts amok : a memoir in verse / Kevin Spenst.
Names: Spenst, Kevin, 1971- author.
Identifiers: Canadiana 20200186183 | ISBN 9781772141498 (softcover)
Classification: LCC PS8637.P478 H43 2020 | DDC C811/.6—dc23

Cover design by Rayola.com
Interior by HeimatHouse
Represented in Canada by Publishers Group Canada
Distributed by Raincoast Books

The publisher gratefully acknowledges the financial assistance of the Canada Council for the Arts, the Canada Book Fund, and the Province of British Columbia through the B.C. Arts Council and the Book Publishing Tax Credit.

We acknowledge the financial support of the Government of Canada through the National Translation Program for Book Publishing for our translation activities.

PRINTED AND BOUND IN CANADA

to Shauna

CONTENTS

Gallant Moocher

Apologia from Hoboken, Christendom 15

A Worshipful Deriding of Flimflam 17

In the Boxcar of Surrey around Guildford Castle 20

A Goatherd's Palaver Clackety-Clacks 21

To Risk Throwing the Guts 22

Summer Crashes High School 23

Cupid: the Duke of Trauma 24

To Buss, Snog or Suaviate in the Language of Yes 25

Éire's Intractabilities

The Blinding Light!! Cinema (1998-2003) 29

Lucky Means Finding 31

The Waverley Pub 33

Hands Held at Symbiotic Angles 34

Epithalamium 36

What Persons Are Fit for Love? 38

Falling Asleep for Ten Years 40

The Yegg and the Queen in the Tower 41

Cuckolded in Schwarzwald 43

Soggy Bottom Boy 46

The Opposite of Face Blindness 48

A Play within a Play in Mount Pleasant, Ontario

Bee's Knees to a Tillandsia 53

To Victoria Park's Glad Rags 55

Lumbering Upstairs 56

When What's-His-Face Met What's-Her-Name 57

Rom-Com to Pemberton 58

As If the *Candid Camera* of Catholicism 59

Quiddity 60

Spiralling Bright 61

The Hobo's Tale 62

Righty and Lefty on the Pump Trolley 63

Padding the Hoof through *Resident Evil* 64

The Word Trinity Isn't Mentioned Once in the Bible 65

Holding it Together on a Tragicomic Tour 66

Disorientations 67

The Summer I Dated Everyone

Another Number of First Dates 71

Saint Maroun Was a Mystic Who Crowd-Surfed
   on the Hands of Date Number Five's Ancestors 72

Lover, Beloved, Baloney Free Kisses 73

The Summer I Dated Most Everyone 74

How Do I Lust after Thee? 75

Read This with Your Device Held Horizontally 76

You'll Hate This Because It Sounds Like a Story 77

Upend

The Architecture of a Rock   81

The Last First Date   82

On the Road of Sighs Around False Creek   83

Above Picasso and His Tussie-Mussies   84

That Summer I Dated Everyone (Part Two)   89

Out of One's Tree   90

The Woman Who Once Lived in a Bus   92

In Our Most Porous Places   93

Hurricane-Held Abodes   95

General Theories of Love   97

Third Testament   98

i love you, i'm uncomfortable.   99

Seismology Counts   103

Ducks and Rabbits Facing East and West   105

Epilogue Logos Flip and Sigh   108

Popping Proposals in the Boodle of Now   111

Afterword and Acknowledgements   113

Notes   117

About the Author   127

Thus well instructed to their worke they hast
And comming where the knight in slomber lay
The one upon his hardy head him plast
And made him dreame of loves and lustfull play
—Edmund Spenser

There are three types of the genus vagrant...
the hobo, the tramp and the bum. The hobo works
and wanders, the tramp dreams and wanders and the bum drinks
and wanders.
—Ben Reitman

Men are capable of Obsession more often than Love
—Sara Sutterlin

GALLANT MOOCHER

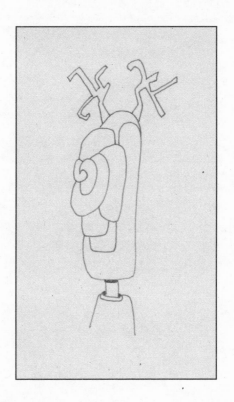

APOLOGIA FROM HOBOKEN, CHRISTENDOM

If my metaphors unmake her
        allegorical gusto,
   gamboling mouth,
      glasses glinting hi to the sun,

    swordswung questions,
        summersault quests,
      tongue that probes teeth or truth —

if she fails to stroll before you,
      glaze mezcal-tinted subtleties,
    grow blueberries from abandoned moats,
  craft sites for queens and guntsels
      transmogrify your hands to maps

          mosey off of her own accord,

you can blame my singsong spatchcock,
      my bindle stick stock of words,
    my tin ear for heeding metallurgy of the dead —

   blame my wingding displays of old flames
   my possum-water eyes,
      my cloudily enraptured brains.

For I wandered lonely as
        a clod, a knight of the road,
      took my sollerets off at the trash can blaze and I swear

she's in a note above odd's bodkins and train whistles
        in a song sustained
               around the jackalope roast

   until infinity flat-lines for broke.

A WORSHIPFUL DERIDING OF FLIMFLAM

Mennonite and Amish women boiled dishes and silverware
after a hobo finished eating. Some may have even feared
spiritual infection.

— Julia Spicher Kasdorf

Midway along our King George journey,
I nodded off in a claggy corner of the bus,
bum-rushed into a world wondrous strange:

a land of scrap metal mayhem for a throat-
clearing Escutcheon-Scraper, and a griffon
grappling a hornéd rabbit at Whalley's corner.

My gaze gathered up the side of the road,
seeking hoboglyphs of a single woman.
I swooned at the image merely in mind

and my heart leapt out as a wolperdinger,
it hopped extra high upon its pheasant wings
bounded down hard on its antlers' shadows,

bolted off to I knew not where. I sang in a fusion
of con and pro while tracking myself into a forest
named "Before Thou Lovest, Thou Must."

After heartless hours, I came upon a camp of
exvangelicals extracting theological thorns
from their hides. They spoke of brainpan

washing, mindset rust, how they'd swallowed
so much of the corpus of Christ; their bellies
now bloated in disbelief. Awkwardly begast,

my insides glittered in fools-gold too, love lustered
in screeds, weaned as I was on post-Mennonite
ballyhoo, chasing goosebump moments around

at Johnston Heights Evangelical where an angel
with a gilt-edged sword severed my sight. I spake
of how dimpled hallelujahs danced round my head

and I would give chase. My heart hopped
sniffed at renditions of sexy righteousness.
Then, under hardscrabble guilt, I'd faceplant.

After a gloss of faith, I forevermore shilly-
shallied 'twixt hosannas and Holy Shits
like a gamboling lamb along Hunger Lane.

After a fortnight, I bid this company of un-
born-again tramps adieu, walked my old lovelorn
suburbopia, past the smacker glimmer

of Guildford Castle towards the skateboards
of Cloverbail. That funny heart high-balled past
and I ran. It dove into a drain at the basement

of my childhood. "Abandon all mope ye who enter,"
crooned the darkness. "Loosed in translation,
the uprooted pipes of yore shall crumple dun

in your fist to flower through your fingers.
This will be your torch to her truth, and forbearance
shall make your cardinal points to one the other."

IN THE BOXCAR OF SURREY AROUND GUILDFORD CASTLE

At nine, Dante was done in by a twist's divinity.
Within this love at first sigh, he upturned a golden
vocation. A map thru exile. At a Kirby Christmas party,
I fell for a girl at four. Barely a blip for a courtship,
we froze into a one-night slow dance in a Polaroid.
Out of my depths at ten, blinded by Maria Gauze,
I blanched. A towering twenty-year-old, she took me
horseback riding. My arms the gladdest they could be.
Soon after, some yegg wooed my sister's friend
away. Heartsick, I sought a coeval, but my fervour bore
a fever that chased angels away. In dreams, we undid class,
pilfered the big bedroom of stars. From shag rug
eruptions, I followed *The Thorn Birds*' world down
under, boo-hooed out the bazoo for unmatchable love.

A GOATHERD'S PALAVER CLACKETY-CLACKS

And thus I see among these pleasant things,
Eche care decayes, and yet my sorrow springs.
— Henry Howard, Earl of Surrey

In those Alpine times of youthful feelings,
our hearts yodeled blandishments of agony.
To make mores worse, I learned in church
that unless I paced a fine line following choice
Bible verses, I'd be dicing a bad-order to hell.
At fourteen, I prayed for the gaze of the new girl
whose mullet jostled like a roller coaster.
I dreamt a Song of Solomon: her cheeks spun
like roller skates in the Whalley Stardust,
her mascara as occluding as Phoenix Metaphysical
Books, her hair, a stage for heavy metal quakes
and pyroclastics. I sweated hours into drawing
her flowers of my affections. Prayers unanswered,
my soul slouched into an iron maiden forgery.

TO RISK THROWING THE GUTS

for J.

Such waiward waies hath love, that most part in discord
Our willes do stand: whereby our harts but seldom do accord.
— Henry Howard, Earl of Surrey

In the adolescent bog of slop-footed failures,
we lugged chainmail to Guildford Castle. We plinked
it apart to joust at the arcade for scintillating
promises of prized maidens. We hid our home life
behind our bangs. I pined for one who came from
Cali, whose eyes orbited another realm; even
off Benadryl or speed, her demeanour delighted.
In the symmetry of row upon row, she danced
during homeroom announcements, laughed as if
out of a *Breakfast Club* blooper. We kissed once.
Her tenderness trellised to another. I stewed, then
our eyes closed to a little square, woke within a pellucid
porousness. Our minds jilted us high and low,
schlepped skuds of diamonds, wide-open all night.

SUMMER CRASHES HIGH SCHOOL

for T.

Girt in my giltless gowne as I sit here and sow
I see that thinges are not in dede as to the outward show
— Henry Howard, Earl of Surrey

After a stroke of dad news, my head plunked on the couch
like a pin-cushion. My tongue an old sock. After a visit
to mouth goodbye, I rode to your cul-de-sac. My sewn-up
speech decamped from your shoulder. A year later, your
mouth enthralled my tongue of pins and needles. My hand
inferred comfort beneath your sweatpants. Our kisses called
it quits. You dated the sculptor skateboarder already
at Kwantlen college, who bowed out early after a final
act in a spackled intersection. Your hobby became passing
out over horsepower. A pantoum sews a melee of lines into
a familiar pattern I wish I'd known. I would have made
one into a crimson banner for our blind charges,
a snapper rig, a reach-me-down for the long wander ahead.
Galoots with awkward ghosts cursing through our veins.

CUPID: THE DUKE OF TRAUMA

For this was on seynt Volantynys day
Whan euery bryd comyth there to chese his make.

— Chaucer

In those textbook days, he aimed for the eye,
a quiver to a quaking heart. Knights crumpled as
auto wrecking yards of screeching agony. Hark,
ManPain! Son of an affair between Venus and Mars,
Cupe'd grown up on visitations with the old man
whose eyes swirled in stories of gore, furor dreams
in which Eros dipped his arrows. Let's sum up
one of Cupid's pamphleteers, the Earl of Surrey:
Petrarch-booster, window-smasher, beheaded.
How blood flowed centuries into a second Surrey
where settlers replenished Slaughter's coffers, pan-
handled rusty couplets, axle swung from a Curley
locomotive. Far and wide away, yet shaped like
a sonnet, here Cupe still coaxed men to holler
hot-to-trot myths from lowdown progenitors.

TO BUSS, SNOG OR SUAVIATE FOR A DECADE IN THE LANGUAGE OF YES

Well give me your lips
Well so I may kiss
Away all that pain
Oh that comes from them blisters
                    — Possessed by Paul James

Smack dab on Valentine's Day after the Student
Council rose delivery event went awry, we ducked
the sharp questions of the rose-less by rabbiting
to a park where I sprung you a flower and we kissed
but you weren't the one. We frenched in Normandy
in a stairwell at a youth hostel after I ran out of *Bonjours*
on the beach, but you weren't either. We pecked
at the Brickyard while a bakehead pissed onto the stage
and you told me about your Wicked Witch of the West
tattoo and your childhood fear of melting in the rain,
but you weren't. We wrapped each other offstage
after *The School for Wives* — I'd kissed you every
performance at your piano, but no. We pógged over
cherry blossoms in the chalice of our hands. I thought you
were the one.

ÉIRE'S INTRACTABILITIES

THE BLINDING LIGHT!! CINEMA (1998–2003)

Seek on earth what you have found in heaven.

—Æ

What gossamer gels held
our windfall at first sight?
After an exterior shot of the cold,
my fogged up glasses illumined
your layers of knittery. You,
a new volunteer at the concession
stand. Posters spinning stars for upcoming
super-8 slacker soliloquies,
a lackadaisical *kappa* in love,
a Happy Hobo cartoon. Under
a black toque and secondhand
flowerings, your lapis
lazuli eyes
washed me anew.

My brains reel-to-reeled your body:
inlets of tattoos, anecdotal trails.
My ear snagged on the lilt grailed
in your voice. An old timey pop-
corn maker nattered next to you.
You'd tumbled into Vancouver to drop out
of art school. That evening, an audience
of eleven or so saw decomposed footage
from a crab trap left in the Hudson River.

Abstract expressionism scratched into celluloid
emulsified my sideways heart
drawn away to the crush of your projections.
Smitten, I gave you a packet of sugar
with my number on it.

> Your one thought through it all:
> I'm not going to marry this man.

LUCKY MEANS FINDING

Since feeling is first
— ee cummings

to plagiarize the syntax
of howsomever — whoever
   fails
      to
         play
              atten
     tion
through the wherefores
       of registers
   will never
      Holy Christ you!

What say we amscray
this square party
and roll
   ('ick!)
       down the Drive.
      (Thee will I praise
past the cornered banks
    on First,
the darkened Café Deux Soleil
     and the hustle
buggies
along Broadway.)   In just this

Spring, when Vancouver
　　rain has a reason
　　　　to fall
　　　　　puddle-
　　　　　　wonderfully on
pizza by the dice and cherry blossoms,

bedraggled petals shall be
　　　　　　unburdened
　　　　　　from
　　　　branches
　　　　for
your pleasure.

　　Let's yank down
　　　　　this night sky
　　　　to rum
　　　　　　mage
　　　around for whispers

　　we'll hold to the soft perch
　　　above our lobes
through night after night after forever.

THE WAVERLEY PUB

A mulatto, an albino, a mosquito, my libido — Nirvana

My star-glossed eyes blotched your figure every-
where. Our mouths slipped origins.
Your first no-nothing kiss,
a boy in grade six
in your other country, as real to me
as Sir Lancelot in English 12. Look,
   I wanted to learn sweetly about every bloke.
        Your first Canadian, a Billy the Kid
            wannabe, arrested
              by the town clowns
        after a gun-heightened heist.
   A fling or two later and you were post-coitaling
 intimations in my arms. I wanted to
outdo these pudnuts, pile euphoria
upon old heart-heightened
trysts. At your concert
in Cumberland, you sang the room
captive. I yowled to a friend, *I want to murder*
everyone and have her voice all to myself. She repeated
        my cartoon longings in clattered
          laughter. As if
             a branch had burst
       from your mouth with a bird
   at the end and I   was the meowling back alley cat
    lapping at the moon.

HANDS HELD AT SYMBIOTIC ANGLES

I forget our first anniversary ergo
out of the blue I cobble violet flowers
and a film: *Omagh*. We hold hands
tight through the last detonation
to blister the distance of your country,
the car-bomb concluding the Troubles.
Hundreds of fields away, you hold
onto the reins of your horse. You
grow up down that rain-slicked road
into Belfast with your Da delivering
tulips within bombshot of new
and antiquated atrocities, splayed in
murals of weaponry and dates,
an offhand heraldry of brick and mortar.

On our double-decker tour, the guide
jokes that the hockey team was named
the Belfast Bombers. At the next turn,
he tears the Titanic a new one. Hand in
hand, we laugh, linger, enter the octagon
of family. The smaller the town, the more
bare-knuckled the graffiti. When the past
churns up, you hold my fingers ashen
white. Later, we find your old yellow diary
with one page filled in:

maths boring
english boring
history boring
riding good

EPITHALAMIUM

And full fair cheer and rich was on the board that no
wight could devise a fuller ne richer.

— James Joyce

Your eyes, hydrangea blue,
suffuse the scruffy corners of my soul.
"We could see their shabby
auras," you laugh vis-
à-vis the pegging of Protestants.
We are both on the blink

from antique beams
of Christendom's schism splintered into
our youth. From opposite ends
of liturgies, we mouth
mouths anew. Avowed lovers
of the clean break, we

repose over hundreds of years
of makeup sex. Jesus double-crossed us
both, but your parents
sold their second house
to help with the wedding, so it will be
Catholic. Accent-crumpled,

your brother reads verse
from James Joyce in melodious manglings.
The Padre understands all too well.
When you laugh,
you liberate needless deliberations.
When you sing, your lashes

brush the air once, your nostrils
bloom, your closed eyes
seal you into yourself.

Blue-eye to blue, we vow
to take down all our hang-ups,
offer the clatter as music
in our forever and ever selvedge.

WHAT PERSONS ARE FIT FOR LOVE?

Not every kind of meditation can be the cause of love,
an excessive one is required; for a restrained thought does not,
as a rule, return to the mind, and so love cannot arise from it.
                                        — Andreas Capellanus

You snore open-mouthed, a glottal
shock of untransubstantiated wine.
In the kitchen I quietly
set the kettle on the hob.

Your dream children scamper
out of the bedroom,
scuttle my attention.
Their voices surmised in your snoresong.

Your shut eyes hide stamps
of their distant cajoleries.
I dream open-eyed,
stevedore tea from the cupboard.

I'll sit pajamaed shift-keying
a search through symbols and vexillology,
wondering myself into words,
attempts at wrestling romance

from a mummified knight
whose helmet bubbles with potato-
water for a panhandler.
How many words have to be spilt

before we're spellbound in the splatter-
spool of another life? How long
do we wander
on words into love? Where do we find

the underglimmer's gawp? I have
my quandaries; you have yours. Steam
stems from a sirening kettle.
Our dream populations split.

FALLING ASLEEP FOR TEN YEARS

At the horizontal end of each day we sed-
imented into our sides, met in the middle to pillow-
talk, bequeath each other dreams. As we sunk
into shafts, substratums of loneliness in life
were filled-in spooningly until one night
I remembered my deepest fears of godlessness,
vagrantdom, parentlessness, and there you were
to have and hold forever. You enraptured me
to my molten guts. The movie remake would
take countless rewrites. For a while everything
slackened out of proportion, cinematically unsound
as I couldn't take my eyes off the big screen that
THXed a vexing end — a paramour charging in
to dismount me as a damn redundancy.

THE YEGG AND THE QUEEN IN THE TOWER

Doldrums
drudge minutes
into your shift.

Squirrelling
in the orders,
your fingers

spigot
routine — a round
of whatever winter

ales you for
ten nontippers,
dead pickers.

Under a workaday-
backache, you serve
in a limbo of blarney.

A new co-worker's
Glasgow patter quipped
from the corner of

his gub. The only face
to confide a shanty smile's
strain.

Days
cashed out
nightly.

Sometimes I'm
sipping at the bar while you
two quibble over

a sawbuck. Sometimes
I'm at home where two lamps
lead you to my arms.

CUCKOLDED IN SCHWARZWALD

i.

Our clocks
wake. We're dead.
They stretch

arms
and legs, impersonate
us for days.

I'm stuck
behind glass.
I can't see.

ii.

You come home.
The bag of groceries
splits, spills

stirrups
stain the kitchen tiles.
You fall

out from time
back to a sort of self,
grief glomming

the floor. The next
morning I am an ersatz
confessor.

How you two
have softened into
each other.

I roll over
with an opening
between my

stomach
and heart
gullibility gasping.

I don't know
what my ears
are doing.

iii.

My gullet open
with halfwords
choked
up

plumes
        from
    an eyeless
bird.

iv.

Our clocks
wake. We're dead.
They sprout

full features
and limbs, impersonate
us for days.

I'm stuck
in a quisling forest
I can't see.

SOGGY BOTTOM BOY

Say, any of you boys smithies? Or, if not smithies per se,
were you otherwise trained in the metallurgic arts before straitened
circumstances forced you into a life of aimless wanderin'?

          — Everett Ulysses McGill

Love is a psychosis,

a cross-eyed
   psychopomp for palookas,

a hobo or hobboett chasing their tale's end,

hooch made to stir
   up the sales around three greenhorns
        boostering stolen land,

liquor that trails one long ago
        lie into the belly,

a myth of us stumbling back to our other half to keep us both
        downtrodden,

a genre germane only to a teen
   from centuries of furies and dragons
       frying in brainpans,

a mealy-mouthed hoarder waiting to croak his next addiction,

an overinflated balloon that blocks
        any escape attempt from its Hallmark Gulag,

a bag of argonauts
        slung over the back
                of Cupid buzzing deaf and dumb
                        for a handout.

Only when Love pretends to be voiceless are they telling the truth.

THE OPPOSITE OF FACE BLINDNESS

Aging for clowns was more of a ripening that just went on and on…
Clowns were born weepy with blubber lips anyhow,
and pratfalls demanded lifelong practice.

— Paul Hunter

At forty a midlife crisis smacks
me across the kisser, as if I woke with Groucho
glasses crazy glued to my face.

I triple blink but kin and kith
have vamoosed, leaving their likenesses
on strangers: dopplegangers with

different hair walking a ganglier gait.
I squint unreturned smiles in the cluttering rain.
She's lost in a bafflegarb of brollies.

Ears rung in gibberish. My middle-
aged insides discombobulate
between appearances and the glare

of the next highbrow bub. How
dare I presume to know anyone?
No one told me what the crisis

would be. I consider the triple
take of loss: a wife, her family, and friends.
I pray to parse an escape route.

In the dandelion den without a floret
of faith, I wait
through the damp blanketing breath.

Accept it. Halfway through
                    we're all bound
up, tangled in yards of pasts and futures,
sitting on our keisters.

A PLAY WITHIN A PLAY IN MOUNT PLEASANT, ONTARIO

Bababadalgharaghtakamminarronnkonnbronntonnerronntuonn-
thunntrovarrhounawnskawntoohoohoordenenthurnuk
—Jame Joyce, *Finnegans Wake*

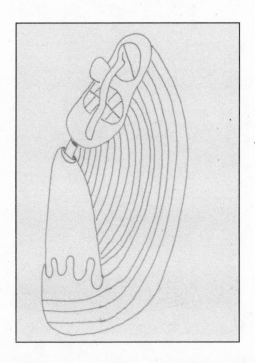

BEE'S KNEES TO A TILLANDSIA

Life is a questionable sandwich from a lost
and found until I cough up an epiphany. Anyone.
The old flirtations bubble up like Venus from
a bowl of scallop soup. I roll up my bindle, bid
adieu to the stew builder and stampers, and talk
out to Terminal City where wedding rings slow
my charge from fingertips to eye-contact. Gin and Sin
at the Niagara is no more and I'm out of schlep
with other dance-floors. Jingle-brained, I locate
the algorithmic back alley where an okay Cupid queries
through the speak-easy slot: should burning your
country's flag be illegal? how often do you masturbate?
starving children or tortured animals, which is
worse? He knows just the gal — she's a house painter,

and an artist, a heart as big as a stampede. Soon
we're candlelit and Ontario flickers flirtations.
Orillia's a seduction of vowels. She studied art
in a Guelph that holds echoes of Dante. Even
the Big Smoke blossoms. She expounds upon
cupcakes: her fondness for fondant as a medium.
Her opinions position her passions feminist.
I nod in agreement, while my hand dreams of
forgetting itself in her silvering hair, opening a nook
next to her neck for kissing. We step out into 2011,
like we've beat our way blind baggage out of the bad past

into a barely believable prologue. "On your first date?" I publish my first small book of poetry to her panache of exclamation marks, unlike anyone.

TO VICTORIA PARK'S GLAD RAGS

The heart is a riddle, a runnel, a game of pick-up-
sticks made of runes. I text emojis to see if you want
to share a small growler in your rubbydub
park. On the tightrope of eye-contact it's straight
forward. We talk until the dusk drops rain. The heart
is no broken switchboard or stuck track switch,
no canned heat with the label burned off. I walk you
half a block to your door. Our faces meet over
the fence of my bike. We shift under the tongue-
shock of kisses. *That'll give me something to think about
tonight,* you whisper from under your hood. You're
movie star quotable even after a day up and down
ladders, your skin flecked egg-shell white. Around
us, cranes reach out as denuded rainbows.

LUMBERING UPSTAIRS

As those unruly beasts to hold without;
Yet was the fence thereof but weake and thin:
                                        — Edward Spencer

I thought of my ex by accident,
a hack job recall that struck with a mis-
handled half-assed hold. A backyard coop
coup d'état with my noggin on the block.
Woodhead me, dumbfounded over double
that it still smarts loud, stuttering out of
the glue — Goosey, goosey gander, whither
shall I ponder? How could our vows break
down in a parliament of vowels plucked,
spat out. The taste of a tryst, bitter
prayers.   A bygone
aria for cork boots. In dreams, I'm separated
from everything   as my head
                    rolls downstairs.

WHEN WHAT'S-HIS-FACE MET WHAT'S-HER-NAME

We met in the summer of the seagull-grey rains.

We met with interest returning each other's lost wallets.

We met in the year of the gold rabbit.

We met on the unceded territory of the Musqueam, Squamish
and Tsleil-Waututh First Nations

We met next to the status quo.

We met as two fortunes inside one cookie.

We met at a Society for Creative Anachronism lawsuit, me
a tramp with a railroad spike through my head and you a king
in hock to a dragon

We met reaching for the same discount screwball comedy that
both of us had already watched twice.

We met as both of us were odd-jobbing
our chops into dream vocations.

We met as two spinning tops.

We met on the third date.

ROM-COM TO PEMBERTON

"Kevin Spenst? He's married," your friend double-
shakes my handle. You reassure him I'm happily separated.
"Are you going to visit your wife?" you slice in jest
a Gordian knot of awkwardnesses. "You've
been served," my wife's friend forsooths as beers arrive
and she hands me a subpoena for a divorce. Uncontested,
it'll be the cheapest route. "That's my sister's old house,"
I say as we park at your mom's. Your nephew's home-
birth befalls the room where my niece had her daughter.
"Well, pumpkin, you gotta light the burner." Your sister
quotes Kurt Russell to Goldie Hawn in a film your family
has gone overboard pillaging for in-house shorthand.
Your uncanny quickness ties together trivia as you drive.
Sunbeams set like credits to a medieval game-show.

AS IF THE *CANDID CAMERA* OF SOME RELIGION

Sunbeams set like credits to a medieval game-show,
a cult hit from north of the Land of Nod where people
confess to a monsignor or a jester and get absolution
or embarrassment. *Salvation or Squat* is the title's
translation. To the English oar, the language waves
like a duck rabbit hybrid plashing in circles. We
are building stories from clouds at Port-Aux-Cove,
our apertures open wide. All our senses awed
from a weekend of snow moondling nightly around
a house at the toe of a forest. The first evening,
annoyed at your supplicant stance over apps,
I passively take my aggressively leave, lose myself
in the mummery of trees. I know the trail well,
step onto parchment softness, hold out my hands.

QUIDDITY

Step onto parchment softness, hold out my hands
and press the hallway walls as codices to down-
stairs. As if the hypnopompic were a training ground
for a medieval woodland in winter. The trick is in
the turn. Forest-wise, shoulder yourself against a tree
and one firm footing, while your other leg glosses
the semantics of darkness. Slow dance macabre,
a vassal of uncertitudes. Remember that in coming
back, branches fly like predators. The snow moans
more. Ask yourself who you're returning to. What
enchantment awaits. Each morning I write a letter
of love to the ideal of you: sleeping or awake; unflung
or far-flung from reality. Kindness is ordinary, but
your kind is extraordinary: heart-blurts in the dark.

SPIRALLING BRIGHT

Your kind is extraordinary, heart-blurts in the dark.
In the seaglass of your great-grandfather's bootlegging
empire, you reign lucid — bosh to the cabbage chewed
away. You've all the bravado of Mae West writing,
producing, and performing in her Broadway production
of *Sex*. You spill big screen treasures. You star
in *The Other Side of Darkness*, not the fictional movie in
a *Seinfeld* episode but something beyond prime time.
Your enthusiasms animate. You unveil daily
the concept of gestalt: sizing up movie plots in
a blink, gas-lightings debunked in a glance. You
have weapons-grade wit, talent in spades and spatulas.
Your fluster is mere exhaust from a driving intensity.

THE HOBO'S TALE

Your fluster is mere exhaust from a driving intensity,
dropping your earbuds into tea, a fluttery-handed
search for your phone, a snappy tone. I don't fluster
I am flust, bellybutton crust. I'm not the worst man
in the world, but I am still yoking together gut feelings
and word flailings. I just woke in a knot of irresolute
dreams, tossed and turned into grainy footage of a hobo
sleeping through a boodle jolt on a pillow piping in keys.
My eyes wonky as diagonally stuck locks. I want to gift
you escapology that's mine in the making, conditional
to applause. I swing under the automatic stop arm
along the tracks. I try on the rails as dentures to hear
what the distance has to say. Imagine our crossings.
What malarky can ride on the patterns we make?

RIGHTY AND LEFTY ON THE PUMP TROLLEY

What malarky can ride on the patterns we make?
A handcar? A tiny house? A Kalamazoo to a family
of four? We squeeze into a Unitarian Church
to find home. Your tears roll over disbelief. The hymns
harmonize in lines jerry-rigged from every religion.
You marvel friends with behind-the-scenes catapults
built for snowballs and suit-fittings for superheroes.
We bundle toss New Years on an island off
an island where I shuck improvised poems for friends.
Mycelium-manic under the moon's goading, I talk
up love's duckets all night. You're worried I'll ask you
to marry me, you tell me later. I'm no cinnamon peeler.
Romance is a trick I'm trying to do with a penknife.

PADDING THE HOOF THROUGH RESIDENT EVIL

Is romance a trick I'm trying to do with a penknife? We
nickle flop playstation for a spell. You now make riffle
in the film industry and a weapon's license will be
equally helpful in the non-cinematic apocalypse.
Zika virus to zombies, the future is the big
boss we decapitate in a crusade to the next
level. The Collapse feels nigh at hand.
Hospice comes in a thought of you.
Practicalities of this outside ride
tipple between hardscrabble
and whimsy. Whatever
our fate, my last words
will be a poem of
a tillandsia.

THE WORD TRINITY ISN'T MENTIONED ONCE IN THE BIBLE

Mini-stroke, vertigo, whatever transient spirit has
railroaded me, I'm living in loosened affiliations.
The (ischemic?) onslaught at the coffee shop: after
I unhand my bindlestick, I still feel the burls pressed
into the palm of my moocher. My vision blags. My arm
baulks outside proprioception. Half my body land-
slides. From the ambulance, the city dragons like
the Book of Revelations. Phantasmagorical me, am I
being reduced to a delusion of singularities? Panic-
scramble to think that it would be at the same age as
my dad. All his losses to a stroke. You pick me up from
the hope-spittle. We stop at my publishers to gladhand
copies of my new book. My sister thought the shot of me
in the MRI was a lark, promotional hijinks. Nope.

HOLDING IT TOGETHER ON A TRAGICOMIC TOUR

The blood runs underground yet brings forth a tower.
A multitude should gather for such an edifice.

— Anne Sexton

Let me begin by mocking myself and my
ventilations betwixt infant-eyed Criminy-
Jicket talk, barely unspeakable spoonerisms
down my throat and Alzheimeric argo bargo
quarterwords that fork up generations of
sweet-talkers. Ergo me, failing to buy the most
basic of linguistic events. My mouth's ups
and downs into migraine outages. But I've shown
consistent promise in how well I walk. Forward.
On this anatomically-shaped Gulf Island, on
a trail that practically sets upon me screaming
with a tattoo on its neck "hobotacular 4 life!"
Instead of engaging in the requisite backwoods
rap-battle, I grab a tree, try to climb its roots.

DISORIENTATIONS

Let's say you grew up beyond the boondocks in a town
which lost the language for left and right.

All directions are framed in reference
to the North. Now, imagine you're hooded

rocketed off into space
by ethnographers studying

your navigational powers
deprived as they are now of certitude.

That's my heart;

it's fallen into the deep space of my stomach
in a zero-gravity thought that you're no longer

mine and hours after we break up in bed,
my body is hauled along in its morning routine

but my stunned mind rides past work,
through the city, to the bespattered end

of space where there is no one
and I can counterfeit a life for a decade,

pick up a few hobo skills, float in a room
without windows or pictures of any sun.

I can fry up some Adam and Eve on a raft
in my brainpan, putter amidst
the exaggerated metaphors I've made.

THE SUMMER I DATED EVERYONE

*Any residual discomfort one might have is assuaged by sentimental
notions in fiction and media that depict hobos, vagabonds,
and freight-train stowaways as carefree.*

—Matt Waggoner

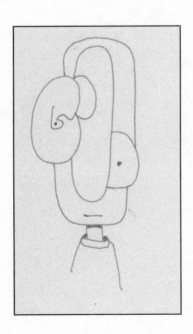

ANOTHER NUMBER OF FIRST DATES

Other men vault themselves trophying a big
catch, conquering mountaintops, shirts asunder.
I post myself as a mime, cyclist poet, uncle to
ten adults, fool-hearted cataracted optimist.
I present unopened 1950s letters from a curios
shop, a bell for her motor-bike, a dog-eared
Charmed Circle for the Steinian next door. I listen.
We huddle over coffee, beers, sushi as my body
jostles intentions: just friends, just a date,
just sex, just a minute, just practice
in sitting across from beauty, just practice in
seeing more than beauty, plings of rip-rapping
bouncing off my ribcage. I'm interviewing
interviewers for the optics of the heart.

SAINT MAROUN WAS A MYSTIC WHO CROWD-SURFED ON THE HANDS OF DATE NUMBER FOUR'S ANCESTORS

She admits the thought of tackling a PhD is a bigger
turn-on than kisses. Her beauty bumbles me.
I turn to look at the sun zig-zagging across
False Creek. I roil in her perspicacious eyes,
lips, cheeks, her mind that leaps through tales
of a law degree in Ottawa to the *terroir* of loving
an addict in Montreal. Both of us flailing for a muse.
We amble alongside under-rippled architecture,
convince ourselves that another date's a good
idea where and when it feels like we've been catapulted
in the direction of each other in slow motion.
                                        I hate slow motion.
We miss.   We feel like a medieval syllogism
on a loop. Thus, we tumble apart as strangers.

LOVER, BELOVED, BALONEY FREE KISSES

(an almost someone always who's noone)

— ee cummings

If pleasure is merely skin deep, I'll dive
across whatever surface you manifest.
Hold out for me a hand and my cheek
will find a moment's fulfillment. Your
arms will be clarion company for a few
days. Your neck ... I neither know your
neck, nor body, so here's where I wing it:
your breasts, belly and back are a murmuration
of starlings; your legs an exaltation of
meadowlarks. Let me learn your eyes:
an unsettling of doves that quickens pulse
and neurons. Educate me in the theoretical,
my pecking order in your list of lovers. How
do I not care? How do we divine freedom?

THE SUMMER I DATED MOST EVERYONE

A Montreal actress gesticulates the stars.
We go swimming, warm a fire with a couple
from Iran. I piece together: *would a kiss
make this even better* in French. *Non.* An event
planner's eyes flutter against the wall behind
me. As if we met on a stuck elevator, waiting
for our other life to open again. A copywriter
from America who reminds me of my blond
cousins so I need an excuse to pad the hoof.
From Wreck Beach, I climb past a woman
on a bench with her eyes stretched wide open.
She's doing eye yoga. From Israel, she's hitching
around the world. We go for dinner. She's
recently divorced. Her name means bird.

HOW DO I LUST AFTER THEE?

Let me count the waves of longing that un-
dulate the length of my limbs. I lust after
thee to a debris of damnations, to a distraction
of delight, a wreckage of debauchery. I lust
enthralled yet hoping to be free, a suitor
unsuited to this foreign ocean of casual depths.
I bite my tongue when the forbidden word
comes into my throat. I like thee a lot. I'm
fond of your blue starfish eyes, your body that
angles in conversation as if flung back by
ratiocination's dynamics. I lust after thee
with a lust I seemed to have lost. I lust after
thee with my breath, smiles, beers. If I were
to drown, I'd lust after thee as a soggy zombie.

READ THIS WITH YOUR DEVICE HELD HORIZONTALLY

In the backyard of my brains is a dig for relics
and whatnots. In the dreamtime before, I rode
in as your evening in shining armour, sweat-
sheened. You're the dragon I adore: flames
threaten resplendence *partout* and sharp green
scales weigh the world wanting as your mind
writhes through bejewelled coinages. You flicker
by your own lights Nietzscheanly, and bring
to boil artichokes. We take five from shape-
shifting entanglements and peel bracts to dip
into rosemary and butter. After the thistles,
we pick up arms — you encircle my last stand.
We crest each other's chronickers. Become
each other. Become pillows. Comely become.

YOU'LL HATE THIS BECAUSE IT SOUNDS LIKE A STORY

Acceptance grows out of the root *kap*, grasp.
Tenebrous arms holding up a lily or cherry
blossom tree. Understand you? I hardly see
you. On Tinder you curated a manierist
profile: underwater, in the desert, up
an escalator with your arms around a man.
Your husband. I swiped right. After some
online cinder-sifting, you found a typo
in my wheelhouse. We met
for a beer, our knees touched. Poetry
poured forth and other old-fashioned things
happened. You pegged me a serial
monogamist. After a tonnage of talk about
art, dance, poetry, I looped around your midriff.

Is this the pillaging excess of lust or the joys
of the body? As if your arms were playing
the role of my lungs. Hold and let go. Each time
we part some alveolus stop. The tattoo of
an equation on your side means "fuck you."
It smacked of coldness "Exactly, this happens
on my own terms." After a *textus
interruptus*, you tell me your husband's jealous.
Now, I go on dates with the world. I bring
all my attention as a gift. Each breath returns

with patience written across its t-shirt.
The store, the candle that smells like you
trips me up into tears. This comes too easy.
Inside is a place called worship that's empty.

UPEND

THE ARCHITECTURE OF A ROCK

with a tobacco-stained anthill
for a heart

— Don Domanski

Loneliness is a boulder at the bottom
of Ye Olde Soul, graffitied upon by know-
nothing punk fears, garlanded by cross-
eyed tourists from the land of Self-Help,
shunned by bum moments. A backdrop
for a Punch and Judy show. Blow out the candle
casting these shadows and let the darkness hold
the glum Goliath's weight. Forgive yourself within
its black puzzlements. Try on its strength for
size. Wrap up in resilience. The sun will rise
inside you in a ringed chorus of singeing, dying
angels. Old depots of myth will be torn down
following this transmission. Broken stones
will pave a way wider than the old horizons.

THE LAST FIRST DATE

"It's extraordinary," says one woman.
"It is extraordinary," says the other.

— Lydia Davis

You rode in with the horizon falling behind like
a dumpled parachute. Your smile landed. Our
tires treaded close to each other. Two giant birds
bequested our conversation with overarching
attention. The sun glamoured in. We clicked our
helmet straps into place, cycled to whisky. From
there, we dabbled deep in chemistry. We'd
crossed paths over the past twenty years. I bought
earrings from you at Dream. You saw a short
I acted in at the Blinding Light. Your heart had
moved you to Mexico, Madrid and then LA, but
these weren't failures. We learn each time, you
said through alchemizing exactitude. We sat on
art made of metal. You farted. *Le coup de foudre*!

ON THE ROAD OF SIGHS AROUND FALSE CREEK

down through the common explosion of time
through the chaos of suns

— Earle Birney

You are as myriad-minded as this inlet.
Even on this cloudy day, it moves in
a million bights, curvatures, wimples, and
when the grey lid over this city slips, light
spills unheard of lines. Each sun-dunked
raindrop stipples a ripple of you. Bright
stories told behind your glass's liquidities.
You laugh in uproarious riots of youth
and your argentium hair flashes the ages.
You're proof cubism is drawn from reality.
You stand in perfect angles unassisted by
any ruler. You're unlike likenesses. We sigh
in accord, play at tug-of-war gazes, fall
into each others iridescent distinctions.

ABOVE PICASSO AND HIS TUSSIE-MUSSIES

to Shauna

i.

Ineptitude's tidings
ashore me, I'm sprawling stumble-
drunk in seawrack

and this grandiose spree of green
beholds an odd bouquet.
Back at the old sandy blanket, our bodies

mold mayhem;
math majors enumerate games
in the indivisible darkness.

During a breather, we marvel at the midnight bay
as it welters moseyingly
under the city of glass' distant subtractions.

On higher ground,
my bed has sprung a squeak. Tempest-
tossed, we let it squawk.

ii.

At loftier
elevations: Picasso and his Muses,
an exhibit we visit

on our friendship date.
Under a thrust of rain,
we give up on appearances and sling warmth;

a False-Creeker
shouts hubba-hubba.
We shroud the light in a beach-blanket.

This is more or less
how it all came to pass. I have no secrets
in my vending machine home.

iii.

Pablo Diego José Francisco de Paula Juan
Nepomuceno María de los Remedios Cipriano
de la Santísima Trinidad Ruiz y Picasso,

a baby soothered in saints.
Fernande Olivier. Orphan. Pedestalled sixty times.
Pablo builds her a shrine. We stand

close in front of the dancing
Olga Khokhlova minutes. Susurrations red-carpet
Marie-Thérèse Walter's allegorized

lips. We almost touch by the Dora
Maar moments under "a comfortable routine
interrupted by World War Two."

We read ever so close, then glide
by Genevieve Laporte who refuses to move
in with her lover, which is what

(she tells Françoise Gilot)
"saves her skin".
Later, old Pablo mistakes

a parking meter in Madrid
for Jacqueline Roque's face. He paints
the parking meter seventy times.

iv.

On our second date
you hold out a gift. I open
a white piece of paper

with more creases than a hundred
hands. It's a map,
you say. Next, you make

a compass from blue string.
This will guide
me through my beachcombing time

collecting gribble-wrought scrimshaw
for a sculpture I'm building to the annals
of honesty hoarders. I'm part

of many secret clubs. You
shall know us by our bookshelves'
blisteringly thin spines.

I should have put
that out-of-order sign on my cubist
pile of a soul long ago.

Some coinage is stuck
behind my five-dimensional eyes,
but I want everything

and you, your mind
of galax, ivy, Peruvian lily, pine,
pussy willow, yellow rose and other

secret handshakes.
You incite objects into a Rube Goldberg
kabbalah, you're a radiance-chain

of life-hacks, embroidery, and Odyssean cunning.
As I work out my zonked
manufacturing to make way towards us

at play. We genuflect
in a ceremony of touching, go gung-ho
into the amalgamating depths.

THAT SUMMER I DATED EVERYONE
(PART TWO)

Love didn't happen to us. We're in love
because we each made the choice to be.

— Mandy Len Catron

How many writs a day do we follow?
What kind of scrip gets us onto the stage?
How do we go off-script without scaring
our co-stars? What kind of exchanges can
we imbue with beauty? But really, have you
ever rehearsed a word? Do you have a secret
hunch about how to live? Tell me about
the most important thing you can't
remember. Is there a power dynamic
here? What if I compared your eyelashes
to scripture? If you met the playwright
of your life, would you throw flowers,
bricks, or suggestions? Tell me, what have
you done to all your polyvocal cravings?

OUT OF ONE'S TREE

While there is no way to compensate
for an atrocity, there is a way to transcend
it by making it a gift to others.

— Judith Herman

He was actively psychotic and in a highly
disturbed state, requiring special attention
for unpredictable behaviour.

— August 21, 1981 (Ward Notes)

Our father was a thirteen-letter word
   for "out of one's gourd." Our father's head
was a hoard of axes and Ohs. I was lucky

        to have three older sisters,
    six soft hands to hold me. Their fingers interlaced
into a nest for keeps. Our father was a sleeper

cell of unhinged voices. Jesus whimpering
        he could help him bring back the dead. In this I was lucky
  to have a mother who stood at the base of the tree

when our father woke with the mind of an axe. She stood
      steadfast through all the swings
   of his moods. In this I was lucky that when the tree shook

I landed with the nest. I wore it like a turtle's shell
     while our mother built a brick wall, and I laced visions
of girls and gewgaws into my green home. Our father

was twacked, an unpickable combination, far more
                    than any sawgosh player.
                              In this I am lucky
to still have my sisters and mother, our unspoken
          arrangements as survivors.

When electrical storms come,
  we swing from branches and sing like windchimes.

          How I cling and jangle longing for love.
                    Desperate for.

THE WOMAN WHO ONCE LIVED IN A BUS

for Shauna

She's a crescendo of jewels, a crinoline spin
a gaggle of giggles in flight. Her pipes pip-
squeak yet her presence is cathedral-crashing.
She's stained glass on vacation, sharp, languid,
shimmering. She's a sunset through a pinhole.
Utopian intensity at work resting. She pushes
her glasses up by scrunching a right or left
cheek and the frame gets the picture. *We'll
have a conversation around that,* she says in
an analytic pose behind paper sewn through
with blue and yellow thread. She bears down
on the world with the resilience of a jack pine.
She runs into me like she's about to dive
into a lake. Her tattoos plash blueberries.

IN OUR MOST POROUS PLACES

Loving is mutuality; loving is synchronous
attunement and modulation.

— from *A General Theory of Love*

two orange
     balloons roiling
          behind
upend   your bike taillight
bottom smooth   at the stop they blimp
pert pick up as   convex acoustics
we mist into each   block after block
other's   blowing
lipslip flower names   unacknowledged
pushed under   nomenclatures
the moon's glad clast   in string as spokes
through   wheeling
plastics of bloom   around thickening thread
into black   you turn

sweat is shorthand braille   yoinking in a tangle
notes to selves   plink of rain
to open the eternal   rising
dawn   our oomph
from kisses   raiment
patchworked   a leg in
zinging   balloon line

and your dulcet   resplendence doubles the city
whatsit lights   routing us home
our new   night turned to day
orbiting senses   lavishing
in   us
              in dreams
with the lights on

HURRICANE-HELD ABODES

In the middle of the journey of our life
I found myself astray in a dark wood
where the straight road had been lost sight of.
                                    — Dante

The house is past.
            — Theodor Adorno

One of your roommates wraps the palm-sized stone
for the bathroom door in orange string. The bolt

lock on my apartment's front door bears a triskelion,
the Isle of Man's three bent legs. Ten bikes are stored

in the basement of your house. There could be more
behind the dead sewing machines. I share a hallway

and a bathroom. My neighbour tells me our building
has the nickname Heartbreak Hotel. You line your front

steps with blueberry bushes and plants repatriated
from outside your ex's tiny house. When I go to take

my ex's dog for a walk, a neighbour updates me on break-
ups, how 112 is now with 202. Your nostrils are serenaded

awake in the summer by the sticky chorus of Linden
trees blowing south. When I cycle to work in the morning,

I head north. Your hematite heart shines beneath
mountains. You write your thesis in bed. You reconfigure

pillows to *go hard* in a tribulation of academics and whimsy.
It's been a year and we still haven't moved in together.

I'm amassing instances of "wait," putting them in storage.
We both married Irishly. Both of them musicians. *Erin*

go Braugh! dranking thru a doomsday ditty. We're both
middle-aged, a term as ossified as the Middle Ages. You

beam through hot flashes. My rocking chair back creaks.
Midway through the journey of our lives we came to.

GENERAL THEORIES OF LOVE

It's my right to wrap my heart in a riddle.
There is nothing between us that is not love.

— Damian Rogers

As we are made mostly of mirrors,
people pair in arrangements
to make the most sidereal ricochets.

Kisses exchange the needments
of wordshapes. We sleep in a boat
built from this sublingual loot.

There's a frog at the top of our spinal column;
it watches over heartbeat and blood flow.
It waits for a kiss's metamorphosis.

Medieval romances were underwritten
by hormones in a teenage oblastland, a harried
bequest of blazoning verse.

The heavens plaster neurochemical patterns.
Think of your love, look up, and witness
the self-same circuitry in the speeding sky.

THIRD TESTAMENT

*There was a groping for using everything and there was a groping
for a continuous present and there was an inevitable beginning
of beginning again and again and again.*

— Gertrude Stein

how edges of pain waver
— Karen Shklanka

To give you my all would be egregious.
An overwhelming superfluity.

Yet, I will pass on this miracle migraine
beginning as remote as an aurora borealis.

In the darkness it brightens jaggedly
without a beep of agony or grief.

It flows open with the tepid tub water
into horizons of wayward rainbows again.

In this landscape I hold the thought of you,
vow to do my share that will bend the day-to-day,

swear I'll live in our moment's making
in all our collaborations' beginnings again and again.

I LOVE YOU, I'M UNCOMFORTABLE.

(performed at New Media Gallery, 2017)

*in the process of constructing gender roles, we are simultaneously
constructing some of romantic love's contours*

— Carrie Jenkins

make kin, not babies

— Donna Haraway

i. Charlotte Brontë in Space

What if we did destroy romantic love? I could not help it,
romantic love has always been connected with the exoplanet-
finding tactic to measure the dimming of a star's light in my
nature; it agitated me to pain sometimes. Then my sole relief
was to walk backwards and forwards, safe in the silence and
solitude of the spot, and allow my mind's eye to dwell on
whatever bright visions rose before it — and, certainly, they
were many and glowing; to let my heart be heaved by the
exultant movement... staring at about 145,000 stars, waiting
for any of them to "blink" as a planet transited... and, best of
all, to open my inward ear to a tale that never ended — a tale
my imagination created, and narrated continuously; quick-
ened with all of incident, life, fire, feeling, that I desired and
had not in my actual existence. But in 2011, one of my four
stabilizing gyroscopes stopped working, followed in 2016 by a
second gyroscope failure. The loss of these gyroscopes

meant that I could no longer remain pointing steadily at my target patch of space, and continued observations of planetary transits could no longer take place. It is in vain to say human beings ought to be satisfied with tranquility: they must have action; and they will make it if they cannot find it. I don't think it's feasible to abolish romantic love.

ii. Love Poem #25

When wet snow in tattered sheets
drapes day after day, down pours
my heart. A Rorschach inkblot of
snot freezes in a cold moment on
my cycle home. Here is an emblem
of my life. Meaning is drowning.
When I drop by, I ring the bell. You
descend the dark stairs. Your kiss
comes as a lifebuoy. Alacritous
clarity. Then, your eyes ground me.

iii. In Silent Revolt

Unless we get better at neuroscience, love is going to retain its recognizable biological symptoms. Could not help the initial exoplanet-finding tactic, the dimming of a star's light in my nature agitated me to a racing heart. My dopamine to walk backwards and forwards in the silence and solitude of the spot, and allow my mind's whatever to be heaved by the exultant stars, waiting for any of them to "blink" as an inward ear stopped working, followed by a second loss, and continued observations of human beings cannot find it. The effect of all this is that, once you spin a gyroscope, its axle wants to keep pointing in the same direction. Millions are condemned to a stiller doom, and millions are in silent revolt against their lot.

iv. Love Poem #26

My app's got cold feet. Where
there should be an icon
there's nothing but dark blue
and two blanks for the temperature.
I head out into the spritzing. The sky's
reluctant to commit. Traffic cuts
the day's accumulation of rainfall.
A stranger commented on FB that my
last poem was suited to a debtors' colony.
I'm hoping for something more in
the direction of uplifting. When
I think of your lips they redden
like stove elements. I love the bite
of your kisses and how they burn
down the background of roads,
registers, and the architecture of kitchens.

v. Pleasing to Laugh

Could not to "blink" as an effect of all condemned to a stiller doom, and millions are in silent revolt against their lot. If you mount the gyroscope in a set of rebellions beside political masses, this is the basis of a field for efforts. More privileged fellow-creatures say that they ought to confine themselves to making gyroscopes with their axles at right angles to one another on a platform, and place the knitting inside a set of gimbals, the pudding will remain completely rigid as the gimbals rotate in any way they please to laugh.

SEISMOLOGY COUNTS

When you dance, you throw
your fists like tetherballs, limbs
oscillate the landscape, and
your face scrunches into
Mach attitude. At rest, you catch
your breath with friends. The world

takes in the helium of your
laughter. Out of mayhem loosens myth,
our primordial metaphor.
When you dance, you tell
me about visiting Niagara as a girl.
You're still small

but when you were smaller,
more concentrated. Imagining your spirit
spins me thousands of years
back. When you dance,
you're the shaman shaking
free of limbs' limitations.

When you dance,
you're storied. One day a god requests
your auguries but you're busy
helping an elderly woman
with her move from a ditch to a cave.
You two yammering like old friends.

In anger, the god thunderously
plucks your body from the earth. Your spirit
holds fast and gushes into
the first waterfall.
When you dance, fables fount
from your eyes. When you dance

you stir up a scattering
of epicentres, a cauldron of auroras
a gorge of feats geologic in real time.

When you dance. Look out.

DUCKS AND RABBITS FACING EAST AND WEST

By the winter-stripped willows
In the park I walked
gold-washed fountains in the
sudden sun

            — Dorothy Livesay

Under the cherry blossom tree in the bone orchard,
we crawl into carnal knapsacks to twist two dreams.
We dive deep, glomming the underground grapevine.
Gravel voices from yore yelp and dump their hearts
instruments. We tune our ears to adventure. Within
one lumberjack growler, we hear:
                                 "There was no beheading.
That Earl of Surrey had noggin' enough to head to
Europe. Took off sonneteering in secret with some
pacifist folk who filtered on down through centuries
of diaspora: Poland, Ukraine, Mexico, to this very
corner of our big ma."
                            We grope through goozlum
for another wishful lineage: I garner fictions
of you having an Icelandic grandmother from Gimli
who sewed a pantoum through winter-stripped willows:

In the park I strolled a softening paradox:
everything is complete, incomplete.
Gold-washed fountains, a paddling of ducks.

I circled my fear buried under rocks.
Sought comfort in distance from the dead.
In the park I strolled a softening paradox.

In dreams, darkness lugged an eternity
stuffed with tender buttons and meadowlark.
Gold-washed fountains, a raft of ducks

helped me see beyond the docks
of this lake, its trails and tributaries.
In the park I paced a softening paradox,

lived inside discomfort comfortably,
celebrated the inferred infernal that roared.
Gold-washed fountains, a team of ducks.

I twigged branches into the shape of a rabbit
set it afloat to sink into this sunset levity.
Gold-washed fountains, a flight of ducks.
In the park I walked a softening paradox.

Not finding any beau in her town, she lit off freight-
hopping in the guise of a guy. Your grandfather had
been a gandy dancer on the rails across the country,
with every jump a lyric leapt to mind. They caboosed
into each other and were lyric-lost, became blowed-
in-the-glass lovers, but didn't want to swaddle on the road.
"So much wrapped up in the balloons of our hearts."

The unknown presses in, shapes us into each other.
Waking from our uprooted imaginings, we head
home.

　　　We live in a dingbat by a wingnut tree near
the pteroadactylic retchings of Great Blue Herons.
Our first winter here, a squirrel stores half-eaten apples
in the branches of a tree. A handful of solid facts
we sprinkle on the ground to bring down the sky.

EPILOGUE LOGOS FLIP AND SIGH

You snore; I write.
The crow cawing outside
your dreams, lands

as a new treetop. Others
shuffle off snow from the branches
of the maple. Your eyes

and cheeks bound and blink.
Snow renders us
wild-eyed in a storybook

morning with no childproof
fingerprints. We make up for it.
Everything present. My heart,

for example, is a wall with a dozen
dogs leaping to jump
out, lick you on the face.

Our building prohibits pets.
Like any bed elevated
in this city, ours was once a patch

of flyway, a commotion
of rushing wings in past abundances.
Let's start a shrine
behind the old milk cupboard door
where we shelter animal whims.
You wake from your dream

trajectory. The pleasure
of patience dawns
down to the ballast, blanket and ground.

Between kisses, your eye holds
the colossal cedar
power posing outside our window.

Trains of thought chug along
past old routes, realms
of rust-anchored hierarchies.

We lay tracks together
from an alloy of old crowns
horizon-sliced light.

We rise and shine our raselbock
embossed handcar,
our three-wheeled velocipede

our mode of thought tracked
in tales of our long journey
into each other's dilly-dallying.

On its side we etch: Let's ease
through love's narrow door. Tomorrow
we'll dawn ourselves again.

POPPING PROPOSALS IN THE BOODLE OF NOW

Let us then lollygag
    and gab through
        the better part of our gaze,
    linger in laughter's sightlines
        and lounge within
        this moment's bed of bucks.

    Let us rove
        the old langscapes
          gauntleting the ground
    like your Saskatoonian BMX rounds
        we'll ride dryers, find slugs for arcana games
        disgorge whatever castles' keep
        nearby the mini-mall.

    Let us remove
        helmets and hennins
        gorgets and chokers
    bell-bottoms and banns
    all encountered countenances
        all the day-old accoutrements of amour.

Let's scooch over to rapture, my Side-by-Side, my dearling.
    We are two and then some,
    a winsome
cracked open a touch to everyone.

For truth turns
        turtle when stated
  and this movement is its rocking
      an edge lowering under windflaws
  where we are blessed something
           tremendous in our tippling forest of flight.

AFTERWORD AND ACKNOWLEDGEMENTS

Here I am in prose. Here we are in another moment mediated through language, but this time at a volume that's different from this book's boisterousness and whisper breaks. As a writer, I'm fascinated by how language sounds as it comes and goes through our lives in lengthy lines, phrasal bursts, and solitary words. Poetry seems to me to be the place where we pause to consider the hinges that hold the whole shebang together. Poets finesse that hinge to its quietest move or multiply it into a crescendo of symphonic squeaks and slams. When I stop to picture a hinge, I see it as part of a door in a house or apartment. Here I am at home.

You are holding in your hands a book of poetry that completes a trilogy of sorts that began with a manuscript whose initial title was *Dwelling Astray*. That manuscript started with a poetic meditation titled "Ballast in Bone," which opened with the short line: "Home is a heartbeat burst." Under the expert eye of Liz Bachinsky, the poem was taken out in subsequent edits. It didn't fit the tone of the overall manuscript, but considering how much I've been thinking about home in the last round of edits with *Hearts Amok*, it strikes me as important to mention. In the precariousness of our times, we may need to seek the qualities we've associated with home in a variety of other places: community, craft, meditation, protest, etc. My ancestors found home in communities of faith as they moved from Europe to Russia to North and South America.

Recently, an age-weathered brick barn in the Ukraine was torn down to reveal tombstones lining its foundation. Since the 1930s, four layers of Thiessens, Klassans, Sawatzkys, Siemens, Penners, Toews and many other Mennonite names from people who'd been born a hundred years earlier had held the weight of horses, farm equipment, and brick walls. I feel a kinship to these names, but I also feel some unease around their orthodox views. When I reflect upon the centrality of love in their theology, however, I see an opening towards something broader (and yes, it's often hinging upon language). Over the past ten years, I've found community in poetry where faith is often an expansive appreciation of the complexities of love. I'm indebted to a very long list of poets living and dead. Their books line my subconscious at least four layers deep.

Here I am in prose to say that I've been writing about home, love, family, religion, and cultural influences for three books now and with my one book about my father, another about me as the son, this third one can only be about one thing: the holy spirit. In my poeticized version of things, I've defined it as a love that matures from romantic pangs to august patience. This book celebrates and critiques the logics and history of love. It's also an expression of awe over the fact of our existence; practical-ities snap another perspective into place, but we return to this awe and wonder for deep sustenance. As poetry is attention surprised into song, I encourage you to play this in your mind's ear cranked all the way up.

Here I am to say thank you at my loudest and clearest to

Shauna for love, all your editorial acumen, and the artwork for the cover upon which I doodled; to my family's unwavering love and support through all the twists and turns of my life; to Billeh Nickerson for friendship and editorial support through an earlier version of this manuscript; to David Zieroth for publishing some of this poetry in an earlier form in the Alfred Gustav chapbook *Pray Goodbye* (2013); to Brian and Karen at Anvil Press for sticking with me through three books of poetry; to Viviane Houle for helping me lift and lull my voice (and funding from the Canada Council for the Arts that allowed for this training to happen); to all the members of my poetry book club who keep me thinking about what poetry can do: Rob, Marta, Raoul, Adrienne, Tanis, Christi, and Shauna; to Pam, RC, and Lucia at Wax Poetic for being rad co-hosts and to all our poet guests who I've learned so much from over the years; to Chelene Knight and Lydia Kwa for your words of support; to Shannon for scanning help; to the BC Arts Council for funding that gave me time to write and refine many of these poems; to the literary journals, publications and editors (Madhur, Joanne, and others!) that first published many of these poems. Thank you, thank you, thank you!!!

NOTES:

Apologia from Hoboken, Christendom
guntsel: green youth (*A Dictionary of Old Hobo Slang*)

knight of the road: A man who frequents the roads, for example a travelling sales representative, tramp, or (formerly) a highwayman.

wingding. "counterfeit seizures induced to attract sympathy;" 1927, originally hobo slang,

odd's bodkins: mild oath, variation of God's body (and bodkin is a needle)

In Spenser's "Letter of the Authors" he states that the entire epic poem is "cloudily enwrapped in Allegorical devises," and that the aim of publishing *The Faerie Queene* was to "fashion a gentleman or noble person in vertuous and gentle discipline".

solleret: a steel shoe part of a suit of armour

A Worshipful Deriding of Flimflam
First appeared in *Grain* Volume 46, No. 5, Fall 2019.

epigraph from *The Body and the Book: Writing from a Mennonite Life: Essays and Poems* by Julia Spicher Kasdorf

escutcheon: a shield or emblem bearing a coat of arms

#exvangelicals: hashtag I first came across through Chrissy Stroop @C_Stroop on twitter

hunger lane: a railroad that passes through country hostile to hoboes (*A Dictionary of Old Hobo Slang*)

In the Boxcar of Surrey Around Guildford Castle
twist: a woman or girl

blip: a nickel

yegg: a roving criminal

bazoo: mouth

All terms from *A Dictionary of Old Hobo Slang*

A Goatherd's Palaver Clackety-Clacks
"Description of the Spring, wherin eche thing renewes, save only the lover." Henry Howard, Earl of Surrey (1517–47) in *Tottel's Miscellany* p.7

badorder: a boxcar on its way to the repair yard (*A Dictionary of Old Hobo Slang*)

To Risk Throwing the Guts
"Description of the fickle affections, pangs, and slieghtes of love." Henry Howard in *Tottel's Miscellany* p.9

throw the guts: to talk freely or too much; to squeal (*A Dictionary of Old Hobo Slang*)

skuds: lots, plenty (*A Dictionary of Old Hobo Slang*)

Summer Crashes High School
"An answer in the behalfe of a woman of an uncertain aucthor" Henry Howard, Earl of Surrey in *Tottel's Miscellany* p.36

snapper rig: second-hand suit of clothes (*A Dictionary of Old Hobo Slang*)

Cupid: the Duke of Trauma
From Chaucer's *The Parliament of Fowls* (1381)

"The first rail line in Surrey was a logging spur built in 1887 for Royal City Mills. In that year the locomotive Curley was brought up the Nicomekl River on a scow." – surreyhistory.ca

To Buss, Snog or Suaviate in the Language of Yes
Possessed by Paul James: "there will be nights when i'm lonely" on "there will be nights when i'm lonely" Hillgrass Bluebilly (2013)

bakehead: a fool or idiot (*A Dictionary of Old Hobo Slang*)

This poem first appeared in chapbook *Pray Goodbye* (Alfred Gustav Press, 2013).

The Blinding Light!! Cinema (1998-2003)
The Blinding Light!! Cinema existed as North America's only full-time underground cinema, operating six nights a week for five years (1998-2003) in Vancouver, British Columbia, Canada. Founded by Alex MacKenzie as a follow-up to his Edison Electric Gallery of Moving Images, the space housed a cafe open seven days a week, a gallery wall featuring rotating art exhibits, a zine & video rack and, of course, a 110-seat cinema. — blindinglight.com

George William Russell (Æ) (10 April 1867 – 17 July 1935) was a seer and mystic as well as gifted painter and poet. In addition to these things, he was also a vocal Irish Nationalist and prolific writer who has left a lasting legacy for the world. — viewfromthebighills.blogspot.com

Lucky Means Finding
hustle buggy: police vehicle (*A Dictionary of Old Hobo Slang*)

The Waverly Pub
Nirvana "Smells Like Teen Spirit"

town clowns: town police (*A Dictionary of Old Hobo Slang*)

prushun: a young boy on the road (*A Dictionary of Old Hobo Slang*)

Hands Held at Symbiotic Angles
The Omagh bombing in 1998 killed 29 people

First appeared as "Hands Held at Varying Angles" in *Event* magazine, Winter 2018.

Epithalamium
from Jame Joyce's *Ulysses* p. 317

Note: James Joyce only married Nora Barnacle for legal issues around his will: Joyce married Barnacle in a civil ceremony in London, after they had been living together as man and wife for nearly twenty-seven years in Austria, Italy, Switzerland and France. Joyce hated all institutions, especially the Catholic Church.

First appeared in *The Antigonish Review*, Number 195 Autumn 2018.

What Persons Are Fit For Love?
From Andreas Capellanus' *The Art of Courtly Love*

Appeared in the *The Literary Review of Canada*, Vol. 27, No. 7, September 2019.

Falling Asleep for Ten Years
This poem first appeared in chapbook *Pray Goodbye* (Alfred Gustav Press, 2013).

The Yegg and the Queen in the Tower
dead picker: a yegg who robs a drunk (*A Dictionary of Old Hobo Slang*)

Soggy Bottom Boy
opening quote from "Oh Brother Where Art Thou?"

"three Greenhorns boostering New Liverpool," first land-speculators in Vancouver who purchased what would become known as the West End

buzz: beg (*A Dictionary of Old Hobo Slang*)

The Opposite of Face Blindness
from *Clownery: In Lieu of a Life Spent in Harness* by Paul Hunter

First appeared in *Freefall XXIV* Number 1 Winter 2014.

Bee's Knees to a Tillandsia
stew builder: a hobo camp cook, a kitchen mechanic (*A Dictionary of Old Hobo Slang*)

blind baggage tourist: A hobo or a tramp that is riding for free as if he or she has a ticket (*A Dictionary of Old Hobo Slang*)

To Victoria Park's Glad Rags
To appear in upcoming issue of *The Fiddlehead* (2020).

Lumbering Upstairs
From Edward Spencer's *The Faerie Queene* Book II. Canto XII

The "Parlement of Foules" is a poem by Geoffrey Chaucer (1343?–1400) made up of approximately 700 lines. The poem is in the form of a dream vision in rhyme royal stanza and contains the first reference to the idea that St. Valentine's Day is a special day for lovers.

woodhead: a lumberjack (A Dictionary of Old Hobo Slang)

As If the Candid Camera of Catholicism
To appear in upcoming issue of *The Fiddlehead* (2020).

Quiddity
First appeared in *Canadian Notes & Queries*, 102 (Summer 2018).

Righty and Lefty on the Pump Trolley
ducket: a ticket or card good for a feed or a flop (*A Dictionary of Old Hobo Slang*)

Padding the Hoof through Resident Evil
padding the hoof: going by foot

outside ride: riding a freight car exposed to the elements

Both terms from *A Dictionary of Old Hobo Slang*.

Holding it Together on a Tragicomic Tour
From Anne Sexton's "That Day" in *Love Poems* (1969)

Disorientations
Adam and Eve on a raft: diner lingo for two poached eggs on toast (*A Dictionary of Old Hobo Slang*)

First appeared in *Event* magazine, Winter 2018.

The Summer I Dated Everyone (section heading)
Epigraph from *Unhoused: Adorno and the Problem of Dwelling* by Matt Waggoner

Lover, Beloved, Baloney Free Kisses
from the sonnet "your homecoming will be my homecoming" — e.e. cummings

Read This with Your Device Held Horizontally
"THREE metamorphoses of the spirit do I designate to you: how the spirit becometh a camel, the camel a lion, and the lion at last a child." — Friedrich Nietzsche

chronicker: a hobo who carried his cooking utensils (*A Dictionary of Old Hobo Slang*)

You'll Hate This Because It Sounds Like a Story
cinder sifter: tramping along the railroad tracks (*A Dictionary of Old Hobo Slang*)

The Architecture of a Rock
from Don Domanski's *Wolf Ladder* (Coach House Press, 1991)

On the Road of Sighs Around False Creek
"On the Road of Sighs" is lifted from a line of Dante's "La Vita Nuova" (pg. 42)

from Earle Birney's "November Walk Near False Creek Mouth"

Above Picasso and His Tussie-Mussies
Vancouver Art Gallery: Picasso: The Artist and His Muses June 11 to October 2, 2016

First appeared as "Above Picasso and His Musings" in *The Malahat Review* No. 203 Summer 2018.

into a ceremony of touching, go gung-ho
Ceremony of Touching is the title of Karen Shklanka's book of poetry (Coteau Books, 2016)

That Summer I Dated Everyone (Part Two)
Mandy Len Catron in *how to fall in love with anyone* (Simon and Schuster, 2017)

Special thanks to Geoff Nilson for publishing this as a micro-broadside through Page Fifty-One.

Out of One's Tree
While there is no way to compensate for an atrocity, there is a way to transcend it by making it a gift to others.
— Judith Herman from *Trauma and Recovery* p. 207

Sawgosh player: insane person (*A Dictionary of the Underworld: British and American*)

First appeared in *Event* magazine, Winter 2018.

The Woman Who Once Lived in a Bus
The jackpine sonnet is a genre created by the Canadian poet Milton Acorn (1923–1986)

In Our Most Porous Places
Loving is mutuality; loving is synchronous attunement and modulation. — *A General Theory of Love* p. 207 (Random House, 2000)

Hurricane-Held Abodes
Dante's *Inferno* Canto I, Translated by Seamus Heaney

from Theodor Adorno's *Minima Moralia: Reflections From Damaged Life* (1951)

General Theories of Love
"YOU CANNOT SHED THE DIFFICULT, MOST STUBBORN ASPECTS OF YOUR NATURE WITH ONE DOSE" from Damian Roger's *Dear Leader* (Coach House Books, 2015)

Third Testament
Stein wrote "Composition as Explanation" in the winter of 1925–26 and delivered it as a lecture to the Cambridge Literary Club and at Oxford University that summer. It was published later that year by Leonard and Virginia Woolf's Hogarth Press.

https://www.poetryfoundation.org/articles/69481/composition-as-explanation

Karen Shklanka's line is from "Sparrow" in *Ceremony of Touching* (Coteau Books)

i love you. i'm uncomfortable.
In response to the New Media Gallery's exhibition "BRINK", poet Kevin Spenst and visual artist/art therapist Shauna Kaendo performed a collaborative work that focussed on the intersections of movement, expectations, uncertainties, trust and the balance we try to find amidst our impossibly complex relations.

newmediagallery.ca

Donna Haraway's *Staying with the Trouble: Making Kin in the Chthulucene* (2016).

Textual sources: Charlotte Brontë's *Jane Eyre*

Carrie Jenkin's *What Love Is* (Basic Books, 2017)

online article: "Despite Hiccup, Kepler Discoveries Continue to Dazzle"

Kevin Spenst's Instagram Poems

Ducks and Rabbits Facing East and West

By the winter-stripped willows...
— Dorothy Livesay *At English Bay, December, 1937*

Dingbat, while being an architectural design name, is also hobo slang for "a dreg of vagrantdom; mooches off other hoboes" (*A Dictionary of Old Hobo Slang*)

ABOUT THE AUTHOR

Kevin Spenst, a Pushcart Prize nominee, is the author of
Ignite and *Jabbering with Bing Bong* (both Anvil Press), as
well as over a dozen chapbooks including *Pray Goodbye*
(Alfred Gustav Press), *Ward Notes* (serif of nottingham),
Flip Flop Faces and Unexpurgated Lives (JackPine Press),
and most recently *Upend* (Frog Hollow Press: Dis/Ability
series). He lives on unceded Coast Salish territory (Van-
couver) with the love of his life Shauna Kaendo.